I'll See You in my Dreams

A magical bedtime story

Written by
Michal Y. Noah, Ph.D.

Conceptualized by
Loren Noah

Illustrated by
Favreau

Text and Illustrations Copyright © 2015 by Michal Y. Noah

All rights reserved. No part of this publication may be reproduced, distributed, or transmitted in any form or by any means, including photocopying, recording, or other electronic or mechanical methods, without the prior written permission of the publisher, except in the case of brief quotations embodied in critical reviews and cer‹tain other noncommercial uses permitted by copyright law. For permission requests, write to the publisher, addressed "Attention: Permissions Coordinator," at the address below.

A Magical World in You, Inc.
Huntingdon Valley, PA 19006
www.michalynoah.com

Hardcover ISBN 978-0-9908394-4-6
Paperback ISBN 978-0-9908394-5-3

Library of Congress Control Number: 2015933856

This is a work of fiction. Names, characters, businesses, places, events and incidents are either the products of the author's imagination or used in a fictitious manner. Any resemblance to actual persons, living or dead, or actual events is purely coincidental.

Ordering Information:

Quantity sales. Special discounts are available on quantity purchases by corporations, associations, and others. For details, contact the publisher at the address above.

Printed in the United States of America.

AUTHOR'S NOTE

In this book I have addressed a challenge that is commonly faced by parents – bedtime blues.

What inspired me to create this book is my personal experience with my little girl, Loren, who felt uncomfortable to go to sleep by herself and asked that we stay by her side as she slept, for she feared bad dreams.

I decided to face this challenge in a more loving and accepting way, and encouraged my precious girl to use her imagination.

I suggested that the two of us meet in her dreams and do the most wonderful things, such as swim with the dolphins, ride on the butterflies, float on the clouds, etc., and my little girl just loved the idea. So every evening, we made a detailed plan; we carefully chose our rendezvous for that night's dream and discussed it the next morning. Before long, she had completely lost her fear of sleeping alone; in fact, she couldn't wait for bedtime when she happily went to sleep by herself!!

My little one slowly transformed into an empowered young girl, confidently using her imagination to create happy thoughts. This truly changed our bedtime routine so magically that the whole family became part of it, and began enjoying it too.

Many poems in this book are a result of Loren's own imagination; my little one was constantly planning her dreams – thinking of new places to visit and new activities to do. She included all of us in those adventures and joyfully looked forward to her bedtime; all her fears were now behind her, which was really heartening to see.

In a child's world, fears are very real – the fear of dark, fear of falling asleep, fear of staying alone in bed, fear of bad dreams, etc., and it is important for parents to approach their child with love and understanding, rather than get frustrated and impatient, for this might destroy the child's self-esteem later. Good communication and a little extra effort from us can liberate young minds from the shackles of fear and set them free, boosting their creativity and confidence.

I've used this positive technique with my own child to help her overcome her fear of bad dreams. I share in these pages the poems we recited and the magical fantasy world we created together each night.

Here's to dreams, and the power of imagination!

Wishing you a magical life,

Michal

A note from Loren:

I'll share with you my story
And you are sure to see,
That within you too lies the power
To set your imagination free.

Each night I asked Mom and Dad
To stay by my side all night,
To hold my hand, and talk to me,
To be with me, and hold me tight.

I prayed for daylight, and even at night,
I wished the Sun would always shine,
I wanted my parents to say to me,
"We're here for you, you'll be just fine."

But night follows day, as we all know,
The sun needs rest, and so do we;
It didn't take long for me to learn
That feeling good is really up to me.

So read on, and you will see,
How it finally turned out all right;
How it worked out so well for me,
And how I created magic each night.

With lots of help from my parents,
Who didn't ignore my tears;
Mom and Dad, you're the best,
You just kissed away my fears.

They didn't allow fear to rule my life,
Thanks to them, I was able to cope,
They opened up such a magical world,
In which there was fun, as well as hope.

Trust me, if I could do it, so can you,
Now, that's not such a hard thing to do.
All it takes is your parents' love,
And for YOU to believe in YOU!

Love,
Loren ♥

Mommy, I don't want to go to sleep,
I want to stay with you.
What if I have a bad dream?
What will happen, what will I do?

I'm a little scared, Mommy,
Please, can I be with you and Dad?
I'm afraid to sleep all alone,
If I'm with you, I won't feel so bad.

Don't worry, precious, you'll be just fine,
Think of happy things, and you won't feel sad.
Let's both imagine that you are not alone,
We can meet in your dream – you, me, and Dad.

Tonight let's meet by the lake, my dear,
There, we'll play and have lots of fun.
Close your eyes, take a deep breath,
And we'll amuse ourselves in the sun.

I'll see you in my dreams, Mommy,
And, precious, I'll see you in mine,
Close your eyes, I'll see you soon…
Thank you, Mommy, now I feel just fine.

Morning, Mommy, I slept very well last night,
I lay in bed, closed my eyes and waited for you;
I met you in my dream, like you said I would,
We were by the lake; you and me, and Dad, too.

I wasn't afraid that I'd see bad dreams.
I was a little scared first, but later I had no fear.
I'm so happy to hear that, honey,
Tell me more about what you saw, my dear.

It was a beautiful sunny day, Mommy,
By the lake, with the water so clear and blue;
We went swimming along with the fishies,
And oh, we saw sea-horses and turtles too.

Tonight I'll dream about you, my love,
And you can dream about me;
We'll visit all the magical places
In the air, on the land, and in the deep sea.

Let's choose your dream for tonight
We'll meet at the zoo, shall we?
Or would you prefer to go to a national park
With lots of cute animals there to see?

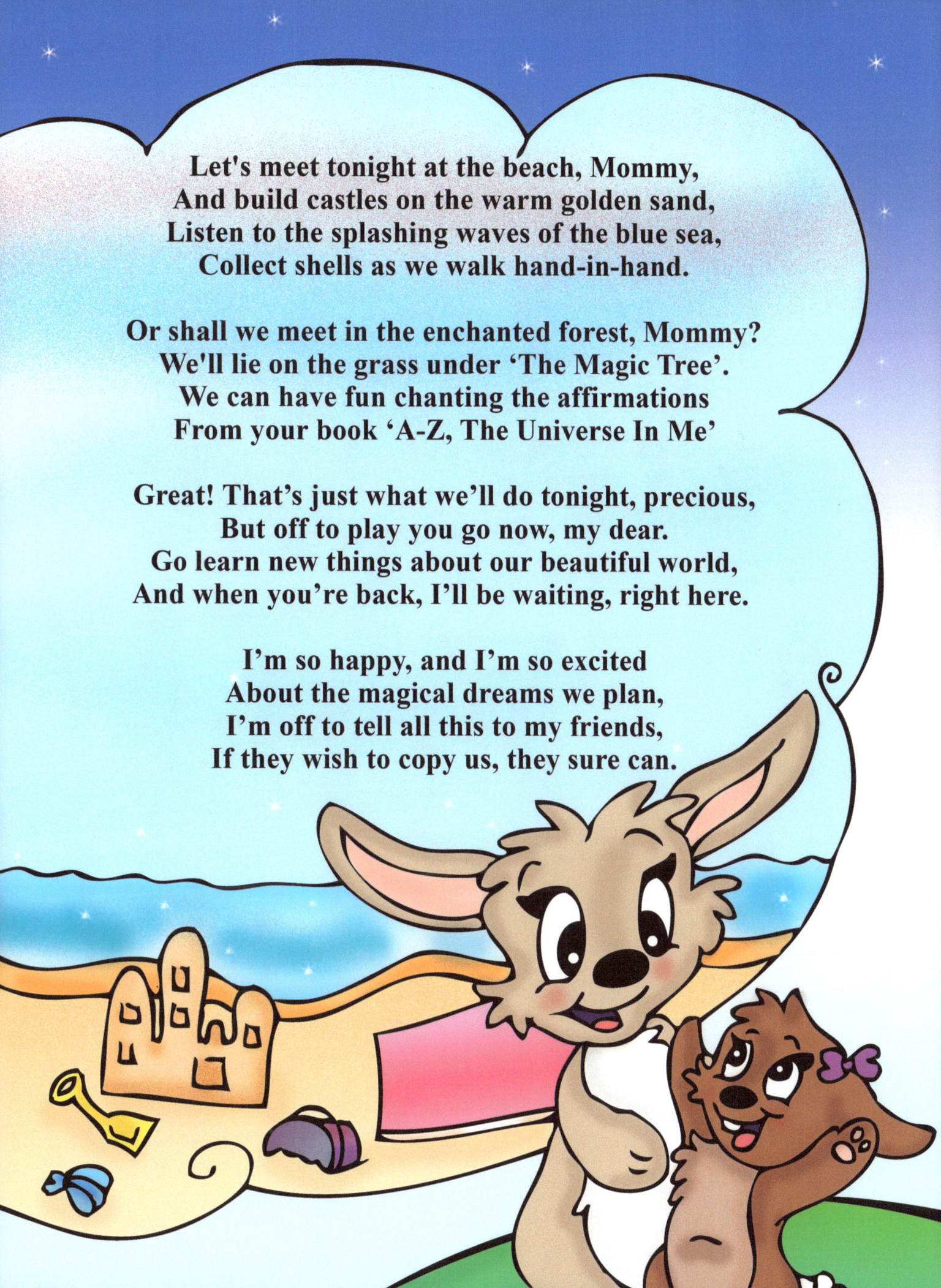

Let's meet tonight at the beach, Mommy,
And build castles on the warm golden sand,
Listen to the splashing waves of the blue sea,
Collect shells as we walk hand-in-hand.

Or shall we meet in the enchanted forest, Mommy?
We'll lie on the grass under 'The Magic Tree'.
We can have fun chanting the affirmations
From your book 'A-Z, The Universe In Me'

Great! That's just what we'll do tonight, precious,
But off to play you go now, my dear.
Go learn new things about our beautiful world,
And when you're back, I'll be waiting, right here.

I'm so happy, and I'm so excited
About the magical dreams we plan,
I'm off to tell all this to my friends,
If they wish to copy us, they sure can.

Wasn't that fun, sweet treasure of mine,
Our little adventure in your dream last night?
Yes, I really enjoyed our forest trip
Meeting old friends is such a delight!

Will I see you in my dreams again, Mommy?
Please say you'll always be there.
Of course, I'll be there with you at all times,
My darling, you know how much I care.

Mommy loves her precious Hoppy,
More and more each day,
Go finish all your tasks for now,
Before you run off to play.

Or shall we meet up in a magical garden
Where flowers can jump, sing, and talk?
Or have a picnic in an enchanted forest,
Where trees can play, dance, and walk?

Umm, no, let's slide down a vibrant rainbow
That peeks from a fluffy cotton-candy cloud;
Ooh, I can imagine how joyful that will be,
I'm sure we'll shout in joy, and scream aloud!

I'll see you in my dreams, Mommy,
And, my darling, I'll see you in mine,
Close your eyes, I'll see you soon…
Thank you, Mommy, now I feel just fine.

Wasn't that great fun, my love,
Our little journey last night in the sky?
I've never screamed in joy so much,
Laughed so loud, nor flown so high!

Yes, Mommy, that was super, indeed,
I so loved our adventure last night,
The rainbow with all its glimmering colors,
And the clouds so feathery and light.

Beautiful morning, precious one,
Did you sleep well last night?
You enjoyed your dream, I hope,
Did you have fun? Was everything all right?

Aww, Mommy, last night was a lot of fun,
Exploring the coral reef with you and Dad,
The parrotfish we met was ooh, so pretty,
That's the most fun in the water I've ever had.

Meeting you in my dreams every night
Is the best thing that's happened to me.
Oh, I just can't wait to go to bed,
I know tonight's dream will be fun, you'll see!

When you feared you'd get bad dreams,
Several times in your room I'd peep,
You used to be so afraid to go to bed,
And now you just can't wait to sleep!

So what's our plan for tonight, my little one?
Shall we all meet this evening at a ranch?
Play with the horses and the ponies
And view the world from the highest tree branch?

That was an awesome trip, my little one,
The glowing moon, the zillions of stars;
I simply loved how they twinkled and sparkled,
And winked at us across Venus and Mars.

Can we fly on a magic carpet tonight, Mommy?
How awesome to see the earth from up so high!
We'll drift slowly past the birds and clouds
And watch as the landscape floats by.

A magical ride on a magic carpet tonight?
Aww, darling Hoppy, how wonderful that sounds!
You come up with such amazing new things,
Your imagination now knows no bounds!

www.ingramcontent.com/pod-product-compliance
Lightning Source LLC
Chambersburg PA
CBHW042142290426
44110CB00002B/93